Daily Quotes

COLLIN MCCABE

ISBN-13: 978-1480016149
ISBN-10: 1480016144

INTRODUCTION

This book contains inspirational and motivational quotes from many people around the World. There is a quote for every day of the year.

Look up the quote that falls on a special day like your birthday, anniversary, etc. and see what insights it brings. Or look at the quote relevant to the current day, or simply select a quote at random and see what inspiration it brings.

I hope you find as much pleasure, inspiration and motivation in reading the quotes as I do.

I use the quotes myself and have them delivered direct via email.

If you are interested in receiving the quotes via email visit my site at http://www.collinmccabe.co.uk where you can subscribe using your email address.

CONTENTS

ACKNOWLEDGMENTS

I would like to show my appreciation for all the people who have helped inspire me to collate these quotes into a book form, including the authors of the quotes past and present. Most of the quotes are from some of the most inspirational people in history, many of whom have helped inspire people not only in the words listed in this book, but through their dedication and commitment to their line of work, interest, etc.

JANUARY

1st January

"Try not to become a man of success but a man of value."

(Albert Einstein)

2nd January

"When I quote others I do so in order to express my own ideas more clearly."

(Michel de Montaigne)

3rd January

It was a high counsel that I once heard given to a young person; "Always do what you are afraid to do."

(Ralph Waldo Emerson)

4th January

"Dost thou love life? Then do not squander time for that is the stuff life is made of."

(Benjamin Franklin)

5th January

"The imagination exercises a powerful influence over every act of sense, thought, reason, over every idea."

(Proverb)

6th January

"I have spread my dreams beneath your feet. Tread softly because you tread on my dreams."

(W.B. Yeats)

7th January

"One cannot manage too many affairs: like pumpkins in the water, one pops up while you try to hold down the other."

(Chinese Proverb)

8th January

"A baby is born with a need to be loved - and never outgrows it."

(Frank Howard Clark)

9th January

"The fact is, that to do anything in the world worth doing, we must not stand back shivering and thinking of the cold and danger, but jump in and scramble through as well as we can."

(Robert Cushing)

10th January

"You must look into other people as well as at them."

(Lord Chesterfield)

11th January

"It is hard to fail, but it is worse never to have tried to succeed."

(Theodore Roosevelt)

12th January

"When one door of happiness closes, another opens, but often we look so long at the closed door that we do not see the one that has been opened for us."

(Helen Keller)

13th January

"If you have built castles in the air, your work need not be lost; that is where they should be. Now put foundations under them."

(Henry David Thoreau)

14th January

"One must be a wise reader to quote wisely and well."

(Amos Bronson Alcott)

15th January

"Take calculated risks. That is quite different from being rash."

(George S. Patton)

16th January

"Life is either a daring adventure or nothing."

(Helen Keller)

17th January

"Solitude is as needful to the imagination as society is wholesome for the character."

(James Russell Lowell)

18th January

"Go confidently in the direction of your dreams. Live the life you have imagined."

(Henry David Thoreau)

19th January

"You will never "find" time for anything. If you want time, you must make it."

(Charles Bruxton)

20th January

"A loving heart is the beginning of all knowledge."

(Thomas Carlyle)

21st January

"The searching-out and thorough investigation of truth ought to be the primary study of man."

(Cicero)

22nd January

"A good deed is never lost: he who sows courtesy reaps friendship; and he who plants kindness gathers love."

(Basil)

23rd January

"Our doubts are traitors, and make us lose the good we oft might win, by fearing to attempt."

(William Shakespeare)

24th January

"Happiness resides not in possessions and not in gold; the feeling of happiness dwells in the soul."

(Democritus)

25th January

"Inspiration and genius - one and the same."

(Victor Hugo)

26th January

"If you do not hope, you will not find what is beyond your hopes."

(St. Clement of Alexandra)

27th January

"Life is like a game of cards. The hand that is dealt you represents determinism; the way you play it is free will."

(Jawaharal Nehru)

28th January

"Far away in the sunshine are my highest aspirations. I may not reach them, but I can look up and see their beauty, believe in them, and try to follow where they lead."

(Louisa May Alcott)

29th January

"Every great dream begins with a dreamer. Always remember, you have within you the strength, the patience, and the passion to reach for the stars to change the world."

(Harriet Tubman)

30th January

"I recommend you take care of the minutes and the hours will take care of themselves."

(Earl of Chesterfield)

31st January

"A man content to go to heaven alone will never go to heaven."

(Boethius)

FEBRUARY

1st February

"The only journey is the journey within."

(Rainer Maria Rilke)

2nd February

"A man's own good breeding is the best security against other people's ill manners."

(Lord Chesterfield)

3rd February

"We learn wisdom from failure much more than success. We often discover what we will do, by finding out what we will not do."

(Samuel Smiles)

4th February

"People with many interests live, not only longest, but happiest."

(George Matthew Allen)

5th February

To find what you seek in the road of life - the best proverb of all is that which says: "Leave no stone unturned."

(Edward Bulwer Lytton)

6th February

"We are all inventors each sailing out on a voyage of discovery guided each by a private chart of which there is no duplicate. The world is all gates and all opportunities."

(Ralph Waldo Emerson)

7th February

"Life is like the dice that, falling, still show a different face. So life, though it remains the same, is always presenting different aspects."

(Alexis)

8th February

"Imagination is more important than knowledge."

(Albert Einstein)

9th February

"Reach high, for stars lie hidden in your soul. Dream deep, for every dream precedes the goal."

(Pamela Vaull Starr)

10th February

"To do two things at once is to do neither."

(Publius Syrus)

11th February

"Absence diminishes mediocre passions and increases great ones, as the wind extinguishes candles and fans fires."

(Francois de La Rochefoucauld)

12th February

"Yes, know thyself: in great concerns or small. Be this thy care, for this, my friend, is all."

(Juvenal)

13th February

"The secret of many a man's success in the world resides in his insight into the moods of men and his tact in dealing with them."

(J. G. Holland)

14th February

"One who fears failure limits his activities. Failure is only the opportunity to more intelligently begin again."

(Henry Ford)

15th February

"In the hopes of reaching the moon men fail to see the flowers that blossom at their feet."

(Albert Schweitzer)

16th February

"If you would create something - you must be something."

(Johann Wolfgang von Goethe)

17th February

"Seek the lofty by reading, hearing and seeing great work at some moment every day."

(Thornton Wilder)

18th February

"Our life's a stage, a comedy: either learn to play and take it lightly, or bear its troubles patiently."

(Palladas)

19th February

"He who has imagination without learning, has wings and no feet."

(Joseph Joubert)

20th February

"All men dream but not equally. Those who dream by night in the dusty recesses of their minds wake in the day to find that it was vanity; but the dreamers of the day are dangerous men, for they may act their dream with open eyes to make it possible."

(T.E. Lawrence)

21st February

"A man who dares waste one hour of time has not discovered the value of life."

(Charles Darwin)

22nd February

"Being deeply loved by someone gives you strength, while loving someone deeply gives you courage."

(Lao Tzu)

23rd February

"Collect as precious pearls the words of the wise and virtuous."

(Abd-el-Kadar)

24th February

"Hear the meaning within the word."

(William Shakespeare)

25th February

"The greatest mistake you can make in life is to continually be afraid you will make one."

(Elbert Hubbard)

26th February

"Happiness is not achieved by the conscious pursuit of happiness; it is generally the by-product of other activities."

(Aldous Huxley)

27th February

"Every artist was first an amateur."

(Ralph Waldo Emerson)

28th February

"The only way of finding the limits of the possible is by going beyond them into the impossible."

(Arthur C. Clarke)

29th February

"The great blessing of mankind are within us and within our reach; but we shut our eyes, and like people in the dark, we fall foul upon the very thing we search for, without finding it."

(Seneca)

MARCH

1st March

"Hope is the dream of a man awake."

(Proverb)

2nd March

"Our truest life is when we are in dreams awake."

(Henry David Thoreau)

3rd March

"The laws of science do not distinguish between the past and the future."

(Steven W. Hawking)

4th March

"Can miles truly separate you from friends... If you want to be with someone you love, aren't you already there?"

(Richard Bach)

5th March

"If we do not plant knowledge when young, it will give us no shade when we are old."

(Lord Chesterfield)

6th March

"We are far more liable to catch the vices than the virtues of our associates."

(Denis Diderot)

7th March

"Wherever we look upon this earth, the opportunities take shape within the problems."

(Nelson A. Rockefeller)

8th March

"There is only one person who could ever make you happy, and that person is you."

(David Burns, Intimate Connections)

9th March

"The more difficulties one has to encounter within and without - the more significant and the higher in inspiration his life will be."

(Horace Bushnell)

10th March

"Without inspiration the best powers of the mind remain dormant. There is a fuel in us which needs to be ignited with sparks."

(Johann Gottfried Von Herder)

11th March

"Govern thy life and thoughts as if the whole world were to see the one, and read the other."

(Thomas Fuller)

12th March

"A strong imagination begetteth opportunity."

(Michel de Montaigne)

13th March

"So often times it happens that we live our lives in chains and we never even know we have the key."

(Lyrics from Already Gone, performed by the Eagles)

14th March

"Time and tide wait for no man."

(Geoffrey Chaucer)

15th March

"Do all things with love."

(Og Mandino)

16th March

"If you have an hour, will you not improve that hour, instead of idling it away?"

(Lord Chesterfield)

17th March

"Arguing with a fool proves there are two."

(Doris M. Smith)

18th March

"There is no failure except in no longer trying."

(Elbert Hubbard)

19th March

"Fortify yourself with contentment, for this is an impregnable fortress."

(Epictetus)

20th March

"Life has no smooth road for any of us and in the bracing atmosphere of a high aim the very roughness stimulates the climber to steadier steps till the legend over steep ways to the stars fulfills itself."

(W. C. Doane)

21st March

"We are what we repeatedly do. Excellence, therefore, is not an act but a habit."

(Aristotle)

22nd March

"Most of the shadows of this life are caused by our standing in our own sunshine."

(Ralph Waldo Emerson)

23rd March

"Your imagination is your preview of life's coming attractions."

(Albert Einstein)

24th March

"The end of wisdom is to dream high enough not to lose the dream in the seeking of it."

(William Faulkner)

25th March

"Time is a file that wears and makes no noise."

(Proverb)

26th March

"For all life is a dream, and dreams themselves are only dreams."

(Pedro Calderon de la Barca)

27th March

"Follow your honest convictions, and stay strong."

(William Thackeray)

28th March

"Be courteous to all, but intimate with few; and let those be well-tried before you give them your confidence."

(George Washington)

29th March

"Happiness depends more on the inward disposition of mind than on outward circumstances."

(Benjamin Franklin)

30th March

"Experience is the child of thought and thought is the child of action."

(Benjamin Disraeli)

31st March

"Work spares us from three evils: boredom, vice, and need."

(Voltaire)

APRIL

1st April

"Life, in all ranks and situations, is an outward occupation, an actual and active work."

(W. Humboldt)

2nd April

"Believe that you have it, and you have it."

(Proverb)

3rd April

"I like the dreams of the future better than the history of the past."

(Patrick Henry)

4th April

"He lives long that lives well; and time misspent is not lived but lost."

(Thomas Fuller)

5th April

"For it was not into my ear you whispered, but into my heart. It was not my lips you kissed, but my soul."

(Judy Garland)

6th April

"Every day do something that will inch you closer to a better tomorrow."

(Doug Firebaugh)

7th April

"Look to be treated by others as you have treated others."

(Publius Syrus)

8th April

"There is only one way to happiness, and that is to cease worrying things which are beyond the power of our will."

(Epictetus)

9th April

"Do we not all agree to call rapid thought and noble impulse by the name of inspiration?"

(George Eliot)

10th April

"If the wind will not serve, take to the oars. Destitutus ventis remos adhibe."

(Latin Proverb)

11th April

"Unrest of spirit is a mark of life; one problem after another presents itself and in the solving of them we can find our greatest pleasure."

(Kal Menninger)

12th April

"The imagination is the secret and marrow of civilization."

(Henry Ward Beecher)

13th April

"Hold fast to dreams, for if dreams die, life is a broken winged bird that cannot fly."

(Lanston Hughes)

14th April

"Take time: much may be gained by patience."

(Proverb)

15th April

"If you press me to say why I loved him, I can say no more than because he was he, and I was I."

(Michel de Montaigne)

16th April

"He who wants, never gets"

(Collin McCabe)

17th April

"Never part without loving words to think of during your absence. It may be that you will not meet again in this life."

(Jean Paul Richter)

18th April

"I have learned to seek my happiness by limiting my desires, rather than attempting to satisfy them."

(John Stuart Mills)

19th April

"No great man ever complains of want of opportunities."

(Ralph Waldo Emerson)

20th April

"Men's best successes come after their disappointments."

(Henry Ward Beecher)

21st April

"Life is short, art long, opportunity fleeting, experience treacherous, judgment difficult."

(Hypocrites)

22nd April

"Imagine every day to be the last of a life surrounded with hopes, cares, anger, and fear. The hours that come unexpectedly will be so much more the grateful."

(Horace)

23rd April

"You cannot dream yourself into a character: you must hammer and forge yourself into one."

(Henry D. Thoreau)

24th April

"Spare moments are the gold dust of time."

(Bishop Hail)

25th April

"If you want to be loved, be lovable."

(Ovid)

26th April

"God ever works with those who work with will."

(Aeschylus)

27th April

"Let us believe neither half of the good people tell us of ourselves, nor half of the evil they say of others."

(J. Petit Senn)

28th April

"There is more to life than increasing its speed."

(Mahatma Ghandi)

29th April

"Men do less than they ought unless they do all they can."

(Thomas Carlyle)

30th April

"You cannot plough a field by turning it over in your mind."

(Unknown)

MAY

1st May

"Look after the pennies and the pounds will take care of themselves."

(Collin McCabe)

2nd May

"The future belongs to those who believe in the beauty of their dreams."

(Eleanor Roosevelt)

3rd May

"The swiftness of time is infinite, as is still more evident when we look back on the past."

(Seneca)

4th May

"In love the paradox occurs that two beings become one and yet remain two."

(Erich Fromm)

5th May

"After the game, the king and the pawn go into the same box."

(Italian Proverb)

6th May

"The more you say, the less people remember."

(Francois Fenelon)

7th May

"Try to be happy in this present moment, and put not off being so to a time to come,—as though that time should be of another make from this which has already come and is ours."

(Thomas Fuller)

8th May

"Let thy words be few."

(Ecclesiastes 5:2 from Words of Wisdom)

9th May

"Do not wait to strike till the iron is hot; but make it hot by striking."

(William B. Sprague)

10th May

"The acts of this life are the destiny of the next."

(Eastern Proverb)

11th May

"Commitment leads to action. Action brings your dream closer."

(Marcia Wieder)

12th May

"Time is but the shadow of the world upon the background of eternity."

(Jerome K. Jerome)

13th May

"It is difficult to know at what moment love begins; it is less difficult to know that it has begun."

(Henry Wadsworth Longfellow)

14th May

"Insist on yourself. Never imitate."

(Ralph Waldo Emerson)

15th May

"Never lose a chance of saying a kind word."

(William Thackeray)

16th May

"No man is happy who does not think himself so."

(Publilius Syrus)

17th May

"Happy are those who dream dreams and are ready to pay the price to make them come true."

(Leon J. Suenes)

18th May

"Nothing will ever be attempted if all possible objections must first be overcome."

(Samuel Johnson)

19th May

"Life is a tragedy for those who feel, and a comedy for those who think."

(La Bruyere)

20th May

"The question for each man to settle is not what he would do if he had means, time, influence and educational advantages; the question is what he will do with the things he has. The moment a young man ceases to dream or to bemoan his lack of opportunities

(Hamilton Wright Mabie)

21st May

"Those that make the best use of their time have none to spare."

(Thomas Fuller)

22nd May

"It is sad not to love, but it is much sadder not to be able to love."

(Miguel de Unamuno)

23rd May

"All that comes to he who waits."

(Collin McCabe)

24th May

"It is always good to know, if only in passing, charming human beings. It refreshes one like flowers and woods and clear brooks."

(George Eliot)

25th May

"It is idle to dread what you cannot avoid."

(Publius Syrus)

26th May

"The power of imagination makes us infinite."

(John Muir)

27th May

"When the best things are not possible, the best may be made of those that are."

(Richard Hooker)

28th May

"Life is like a library owned by the author. In it are a few books which he wrote himself, but most of them were written for him."

(Harry Emerson Fosdick)

29th May

"The best way to make your dreams come true is to wake up."

(Paul Valery)

30th May

"To comprehend a man's life, it is necessary to know not merely what he does but also what he purposely leaves undone. There is a limit to the work that can be got out of a human body or a human brain, and he is a wise man who wastes no energy on pursuits

(John Hall Gladstone)

31st May

"Love is a game that two can play and both win."

(Eva Gabor)

JUNE

1st June

"Knowing yourself is the beginning of all wisdom."

(Aristotle)

2nd June

"If evil be said of thee, and if it be true, correct thyself; if it be a lie, laugh at it."

(Epictetus)

3rd June

"First say to yourself what you would be and then do what you have to do."

(Epictetus)

4th June

"He who hesitates is lost."

(Unknown)

5th June

"The best way to prepare for life is to begin to live."

(Elbert Hubbard)

6th June

"A skillful man reads his dreams for self-knowledge, yet not the details but the quality."

(Ralph Waldo Emerson)

7th June

"Time, which changes people, does not alter the image we have of them."

(Marcel Proust)

8th June

"Love is composed of a single soul inhabiting two bodies."

(Aristotle)

9th June

"Our ideas, like orange-plants, spread out in proportion to the size of the box which imprisons the roots."

(Edward Bulwer Lytton)

10th June

"The less people speak of their greatness, the more we think of it."

(Lord Bacon)

11th June

"Be silent or say something better than silence."

(Pythagoras)

12th June

"Great spirits have always encountered violent opposition from mediocre minds."

(Albert Einstein)

13th June

"Life's a voyage that's homeward bound."

(Herman Melville)

14th June

"Our waking hours form the text of our lives, our dreams, the commentary."

(Anonymous)

15th June

"Time is a physician which heals every grief."

(Diphilus)

16th June

"Love takes off masks that we fear we cannot live without and know we cannot live within."

(James A. Baldwin)

17th June

"In learning to know other things, and other minds, we become more intimately acquainted with ourselves, and are to ourselves better worth knowing."

(Philip Gilbert Hamilton)

18th June

"He who sedulously attends, pointedly asks, calmly speaks, coolly answers and ceases when he has no more to say is in possession of some of the best requisites of man."

(Johann Casper Lavater)

19th June

"Proper words in proper places make the true definition of a style."

(Jonathan Swift)

20th June

"Knowing is not enough; we must apply. Willing is not enough; we must do."

(Johann Wolfgang von Goethe)

21st June

"The whole of life is but a moment of time. It is our duty, therefore to use it, not to misuse it."

(Plutarch)

22nd June

"To unpathed waters, undreamed shores."

(William Shakespeare)

23rd June

"Gaining time is gaining everything in love, trade and war."

(John Shebbeare)

24th June

"Nothing is miserable unless you think it is so."

(Boethius)

25th June

"We are either progressing or retrograding all the while; there is no such thing as remaining stationary in this life."

(James Freeman Clarke)

26th June

"It is as easy to draw back a stone thrown with force from the hand as to recall a word once spoken."

(Menander)

27th June

"We are still masters of our fate. We are still captains of our souls."

(Winston Churchill)

28th June

"Life is a rich strain of music, suggesting a realm too fair to be."

(George William Curtis)

29th June

"The more business a man has to do, the more he is able to accomplish, for he learns to economize his time."

(Sir Matthew Hale)

30th June

"Sometimes the heart sees what is invisible to the eye."

(H. Jackson Brown, Jr.)

JULY

1st July

"The happiest life is that which constantly exercises and educates what is best in us."

(Hamerton)

2nd July

"Much tongue and much judgment seldom go together."

(Roger L'Estrange)

3rd July

"Nothing great was ever achieved without enthusiasm."

(Ralph Waldo Emerson)

4th July

"The boundaries which divide life from death are at best shadowy and vague. Who shall say where one ends, and the other begins?"

(Edgar Alan Poe)

5th July

"Time is but the stream I go a-fishin in."

(Henry David Thoreau)

6th July

"The moment you have in your heart this extraordinary thing called love and feel the depth, the delight, the ecstasy of it, you will discover that for you the world is transformed."

(Jiddu Krishnamurti)

7th July

"We only become what we are by the radical and deep-seated refusal of that which others have made of us."

(Jean-Paul Sartre)

8th July

"If the truth were self-evident eloquence would be unnecessary."

(Cicero)

9th July

"For hope is but the dream of those that wake."

(Matthew Prior)

10th July

"One way to get the most out of life is to look upon it as an adventure."

(William Feather)

11th July

"He who know most grieves most for wasted time."

(Dante)

12th July

"We are not the same persons this year as last; nor are those we love. It is a happy chance if we, changing, continue to love a changed person."

(W. Somerset Maugham)

13th July

"Change and growth take place when a person has risked himself and dares to become involved with experimenting with his own life."

(Otto)

14th July

"We never listen when we are eager to speak."

(François de La Rochefoucauld)

15th July

"Constant dripping hollows out a stone."

(Lucretius)

16th July

"Life is a succession of lessons which must be lived to be understood."

(Ralph Waldo Emerson)

17th July

"Heed the still small voice that so seldom leads us wrong, and never into folly."

(Marquise du Deffand)

18th July

"He that converses not knows nothing."

(English Proverb)

19th July

"Nothing contributes so much to tranquilize the mind as a steady purpose - a point on which the soul may fix its intellectual eye."

(Mary Shelley)

20th July

"Obstacles are what we see when we take our eye off the goal."

(Collin McCabe)

21st July

"Your real influence is measured by your treatment of yourself."

(A. Bronson Alcott)

22nd July

"It is good to rub and polish our brain against that of others."

(Montaigne)

23rd July

"Heaven ne'er helps the man who will not help himself."

(Sophocles)

24th July

"To live is like to love - all reason is against it, and all healthy instinct for it."

(Samuel Butler)

25th July

"If we all did the things we are capable of we would astound ourselves."

(Thomas Edison)

26th July

"My words fly up my thoughts remain below - Words without thoughts never to heaven go."

(William Shakespeare - Hamlet. Act III. Sc. 3)

27th July

"The journey of a thousand miles begins with a single step."

(Lao Tzu)

28th July

"One life - a little gleam of time between two eternities."

(Thomas Carlyle)

29th July

"A man who finds no satisfaction in himself will seek for it in vain elsewhere."

(La Rochefoucauld)

30th July

"Kind words are the music of the world."

(F. W. Faber)

31st July

"Industry is the parent of success."

(Spanish Proverb)

AUGUST

1st August

"Life is a pure flame and we live by an invisible sun within us."

(Sir Thomas Brown)

2nd August

"Fear less, hope more, eat less, chew more, whine less, breathe more, talk less, say more, hate less, love more, and good things will be yours."

(Proverb)

3rd August

"People who have nothing to say are never at a loss in talking."

(Josh Bilings)

4th August

"Thought is the seed of action."

(Ralph Waldo Emerson)

5th August

"In prosperity, our friends know us; in adversity, we know our friends."

(John Churton Collins)

6th August

"Make it thy business to know thyself, which is the most difficult lesson in the world."

(Miguel de Cervantes)

7th August

"Deliver your words not by number but by weight."

(Proverb)

8th August

"What lies behind us and what lies before us are tiny matters compared to what lies within us."

(Ralph Waldo Emerson)

9th August

"The obstacles of your past can become the gateways that lead to new beginnings."

(Ralph Blum)

10th August

"Exert your talents, and distinguish yourself, and don't think of retiring from the world, until the world will be sorry that you retire."

(Samuel Johnson)

11th August

"The great thing is to know when to speak and when to keep quiet."

(Seneca the Younger)

12th August

"Self-trust is the first secret of success."

(Ralph Waldo Emerson)

13th August

"It has been my philosophy of life that difficulties vanish when faced boldly."

(Isaac Asimov)

14th August

"Employ your time in improving yourself by other men's writings so that you shall come easily by what others have labored hard for."

(Socrates)

15th August

"Silence is often advantageous."

(Menander)

16th August

"When it is dark enough, you can see the stars."

(Persian Proverb)

17th August

"Good fortune and bad are equally necessary to man, to fit him to meet the contingencies of this life."

(Proverb)

18th August

"People seldom improve when they have no other model but themselves to copy."

(Oliver Goldsmith)

19th August

"Many can argue - not many converse."

(A. Bronson Alcott)

20th August

"You must know for which harbor you are headed if you are to catch the right wind to take you there."

(Seneca)

21st August

"It is interesting to notice how some minds seem almost to create themselves, springing up under every disadvantage, and working their solitary but irresistible way through a thousand obstacles."

(Washington Irving)

22nd August

"The safest principle through life, instead of reforming others, is to set about perfecting yourself."

(B. R. Haydon)

23rd August

"The less people speak of their greatness the more we think of it."

(Sir Francis Bacon)

24th August

"Lots of things that couldn't be done have been done."

(Charles Auston Bates)

25th August

"The man of virtue makes the difficulty to be overcome his first business, and success only a subsequent consideration."

(Confucius)

26th August

"What you dislike in another take care to correct in yourself."

(Thomas Sprat)

27th August

"Language is the close-fitting dress of Thought."

(R. C. Trench)

28th August

"The winds and the waves are always on the side of the ablest navigators."

(Edward Gibbon)

29th August

"All misfortune is but a stepping stone to fortune."

(Henry David Thoreau)

30th August

"The highest purpose of intellectual cultivation is to give a man a perfect knowledge and mastery of his own inner self; to render our consciousness its own light and its own mirror."

(Frederich Leopold von Hardenberg)

31st August

"'Good' the more communicated - more abundant grows."

(John Milton)

SEPTEMBER

1st September

"They can conquer who believe they can."

(Ralph Waldo Emerson)

2nd September

"Fractures well cured make us more strong."

(Ralph Waldo Emerson)

3rd September

"In this world man must either be anvil or hammer."

(Henry W. Longfellow)

4th September

"The first ingredient in conversation is truth: the next good sense; the third good humor; and the fourth wit."

(Sir William Temple)

5th September

"There are glimpses of heaven to us in every act, or thought, or word that raises us above ourselves."

(A. P. Stanley)

6th September

"Misfortunes often sharpen the genius."

(Ovid)

7th September

"What are the aims which are at the same time duties? They are perfecting of ourselves, the happiness of others."

(Immanuel Kant)

8th September

"Be not afraid of greatness: some are born great, some achieve greatness, and some have greatness thrust upon them."

(William Shakespeare)

9th September

"Success in the affairs of life often serves to hide one's abilities, whereas adversity frequently gives one an opportunity to discover them."

(Horace)

10th September

"Many only learns in two ways, one by reading, and the other by association with smarter people."

(Will Rogers)

11th September

"Skill and confidence are an unconquered army."

(George Herbert)

12th September

"Look not mournfully into the past, it comes not back again. Wisely improve the present, it is thine. Go forth to meet the shadowy future without fear and with a manly heart."

(Henry Wadsworth Longfellow)

13th September

"Every man has in himself a continent of undiscovered character. Happy is he who acts as the Columbus to his own soul."

(Sir J. Stephen)

14th September

"If you aren't going all the way, why go at all?"

(Joe Namath)

15th September

"A gentleman can withstand hardships; it is only the small man who, when submitted to them, is swept off his feet."

(Confucius)

16th September

"Discontent is the source of all trouble but also of all progress in individuals and nations."

(Berthold Auerbach)

17th September

"Victory belongs to the most persevering."

(Napoleon Bonaparte)

18th September

"Little minds are tamed and subdued by misfortune, but great minds rise above them."

(Washington Irving)

19th September

"Slumber not in the tents of your fathers! The world is advancing. Advance with it!"

(Mazzini)

20th September

"You are the handicap you must face. You are the one who must choose your place."

(James Lane Allen)

21st September

"Difficulties strengthen the mind as well as labour does the body."

(Seneca)

22nd September

"The greatest of faults is to be conscious of none."

(Thomas Carlyle)

23rd September

"Sports serve society by providing vivid examples of excellence."

(George F. Will)

24th September

"Times of great calamity and confusion have ever been productive of the greatest minds. The purest ore is produced from the hottest furnace, and the brightest thunderbolt is elicited from the darkest storm."

(Charles Caleb Colton)

25th September

"Hold yourself responsible for a higher standard than anyone else expects of you. Never excuse yourself."

(Henry Ward Beecher)

26th September

"There are no gains without pains."

(Adlai Stevenson)

27th September

"The gem cannot be polished without friction, nor man be perfected without trials."

(Proverb)

28th September

"Remedy your deficiencies and your merits will take care of themselves."

(Edward Bulwer-Lytton)

29th September

"If at first you don't succeed, try, try again."

(William Edward Hickson)

30th September

"Obstacles are great incentives."

(Jules Michelet)

OCTOBER

1st October

"Look within, for within is the wellspring of virtue which will not cease flowing if you cease not from digging."

(Marcus Aurelius)

2nd October

"To win without risk is to triumph without glory."

(Corneille)

3rd October

"There are no classes in life for beginners: right away you are always asked to deal with what is most difficult."

(Rainer Maria Rilke)

4th October

"Everyone has naturally the power of excelling in some one thing."

(Proverb)

5th October

"They can because they think they can."

(Virgil)

6th October

"In the midst of winter, I found there was within me an invincible summer."

(Albert Careb)

7th October

"Practice yourself in little things, and thence proceed to greater."

(Epictetus)

8th October

"They will rise highest who strive for the highest place. (Altius ibunt qui as summa nituntur)"

(Latin Proverb)

9th October

"A wise man adapts himself to circumstances as water shapes itself to the vessel that contains it."

(Chinese Proverb)

10th October

"If you have great talents, industry will improve them; If moderate abilities, industry will supply their deficiencies. Nothing is denied to well-directed labor: nothing is ever to be attained without it."

(Sir Joshua Reynolds)

11th October

"Never say die."

(Proverb)

12th October

"Persistent people begin their success where others end in failure."

(Edward Eggleston)

13th October

"There is nothing noble about being superior to some other man. The true nobility is in being superior to your previous self."

(Hindu Proverb)

14th October

"It isn't hard to be good from time to time. What's tough is being good every day."

(Willie Mays)

15th October

"Problems are only opportunities in work clothes."

(Henry J. Kaiser)

16th October

"What you are must always displease you, if you would attain to that which you are not."

(Saint Augustine)

17th October

"You are never a loser until you quit trying."

(Mike Ditka)

18th October

"What is defeat? Nothing but education; nothing but the first steps to something better."

(Proverb)

19th October

"We think too small. Like the frog at the bottom of the well. He thinks the sky is only as big as the top of the well. If he surfaced, he would have an entirely different view."

(Mao Tse-Tung)

20th October

"If you can't accept losing, you can't win."

(Vince Lombardi)

21st October

"Sweet are the uses of adversity, which like the toad, ugly and venomous, Wears yet a precious jewel in his head."

(William Shakespeare)

22nd October

"Thoughts are but dreams till their effects be tried."

(William Shakespeare)

23rd October

"Nothing succeeds like success."

(Proverb)

24th October

"It is the surmounting of difficulties that make heroes."

(Louis Kossuth)

25th October

"Men give me some credit for genius. All the genius I have lies in this: When I have a subject in hand, I study it profoundly. Day and night it is before me. I explore it in all its bearings. My mind becomes pervaded with it. Then the effort which I make

(Alexander Hamilton)

26th October

"Our greatest glory consists not in never falling, but in rising every time we fall."

(Confucius)

27th October

"Wherever we look upon this earth, the opportunities take shape within the problems."

(Nelson A. Rockefeller)

28th October

"The aim of education should be to teach us how to think, rather than what to think."

(James Beattie)

29th October

"The block of granite which was an obstacle in the pathway of the weak, became a stepping-stone in the pathway of the strong."

(Thomas Carlyle)

30th October

"Prosperity is a great teacher; adversity a greater."

(William Hazlitt)

31st October

"Believe whatever you choose to believe. But whatever is, is"

(Collin McCabe)

NOVEMBER

1st November

"Press on! A better fate awaits thee."

(Victor Hugo)

2nd November

"Difficulties, by bracing the mind to overcome them, assist cheerfulness, as exercise assists digestion."

(Christian Nestell Bovee)

3rd November

"All truly wise thoughts have been thought already, thousands of times; but to make them truly ours, we must think them over again honestly, till they take firm root in our personal experience."

(Johann Wolfgang von Goethe)

4th November

"The waters wear the stones."

(The Book of Job 14:19)

5th November

"Experience is a grindstone; and it is lucky for us, if we can get brightened by it, and not ground."

(Josh Billings)

6th November

"The universe is change; our life is what our thoughts make it."

(Marcus Aurelius)

7th November

"Energy and persistence conquer all things."

(Benjamin Franklin)

8th November

"Experience is by industry achieved, and perfected by the swift course of time."

(William Shakespeare)

9th November

"But words are things, and a small drop of ink falling like dew upon a thought, produces that which makes thousands, perhaps millions, think."

(Sir Aubrey De Vere)

10th November

"The man who removes a mountain begins by carrying away small stones."

(Chinese Proverb)

11th November

"Experience keeps a dear school, but fools will learn in no other, and scarce in that; for it is true we may give advice, but we cannot give conduct."

(Benjamin Franklin)

12th November

"Thinking is the talking of the soul with itself."

(Plato)

13th November

"Nothing great is created suddenly, any more than a bunch of grapes or a fig."

(Epictetus)

14th November

"The education of circumstances is superior to that of tuition."

(William Wordsworth)

15th November

"Change your thoughts and you change your world."

(Norman Vincent Peale)

16th November

"The important thing in life is to have great aim and to possess the aptitude and the perseverance to attain it."

(Johann Wolfgang Von Goethe)

17th November

"It is good to learn what to avoid by studying the misfortunes of others."

(Publius Syrius)

18th November

"Obvious thinking commonly leads to wrong judgments and wrong conclusions."

(Humphrey B. Neil)

19th November

"Success in life is a matter not so much of talent or opportunity as of concentration and perseverance."

(C. W. Wendte)

20th November

"The experience of others adds to our knowledge, but not to our wisdom; that is dearer bought."

(Hosea Ballou)

21st November

"Those who would attain to any marked degree of excellence in a chosen pursuit must work, and work hard for it."

(Bayard Taylor)

22nd November

"He knows the water best who has waded through it."

(Proverb)

23rd November

"It is interesting to notice how some minds seem almost to create themselves, springing up under every disadvantage, and working their solitary but irresistible way through a thousand obstacles."

(Washington Irving)

24th November

"If you would like to know the road ahead, ask someone who has traveled it."

(Chinese Proverb)

25th November

"Let me tell you the secret that has led me to my goal. My strength lies solely in my tenacity."

(Louis Pasteur)

26th November

"The years teach much which the days never know."

(Ralph Waldo Emerson)

27th November

"Sometimes in life we need to experience the dark in order to appreciate the light"

(Collin McCabe)

28th November

"All experience is an arch to build upon."

(Henry Brook Adams)

29th November

"The drops of rain make a hole in the stone, not by violence, but by oft falling."

(Lucretius 95 BC - From Perseverance)

30th November

"Experience is a jewel, and it had need be so, for it is often purchased at an infinite rate."

(William Shakespeare)

DECEMBER

1st December

"He who would do some great thing in this short life, must apply himself to the work with such a concentration of his forces as to the idle spectators, who live only to amuse themselves, looks like insanity."

(John Foster)

2nd December

"Experience is a safe light to walk by, and he is not a rash man who expects to succeed in future from the same means which have secured it in times past."

(Wendell Phillips)

3rd December

"Do not think that what is hard for thee to master is impossible for man; but if a thing is possible and proper to man, deem it attainable by thee."

(Marcus Aurelius)

4th December

"Pick up a grain a day and add to your heap. You will soon learn, by happy experience, the power of littles as applied to intellectual processes and gains."

(John S. Hart)

5th December

"It does not matter how slowly you go so long as you do not stop."

(Confucius)

6th December

"A moment's insight is sometimes worth a life's experience."

(Oliver Wendall Holmes)

7th December

"The fact is that in order to do anything in this world worth doing, we must not stand shivering on the bank thinking of the cold and the danger, but jump in and scramble through as well as we can."

(Sydney Smith)

8th December

"Experience is not what happens to a man: it is what a man does with what happens to him."

(Aldous Huxley)

9th December

"There are three kinds of people in the world, the wills, the wont's and the cant's. The first accomplish everything; the second oppose everything; the third fail in everything."

(Eclectic Magazine)

10th December

"Experience is the child of thought, and thought is the child of action. We cannot learn men from books."

(Benjamin Disraeli)

11th December

"Success does not consist in never making blunders, but in never making the same one the second time."

(H. W. Shaw)

12th December

"You are what your deep, driving desire is. As your desire is, so is your will. As your will is, so is your deed. As your deed is, so is your destiny."

(Brihadaranyaka Upanishad IV 4.5)

13th December

"There is no royal road to anything. One thing at a time, all things in succession. That which grows fast, withers as rapidly. That which grows slowly, endures."

(Josiah Gilbert Holland)

14th December

"If we would see the color of our future, we must look for it in our present; if we would gaze on the star of our destiny, we must look for it in our hearts."

(Canon Farrar)

15th December

"The great thing in this world is not so much where you stand, as in what direction you are moving."

(Oliver Wendell Holmes)

16th December

"Everywhere man blames nature and fate, yet his fate is mostly but the echo of his character and passions, his mistakes and weaknesses."

(Democritus)

17th December

"Either attempt it not, or succeed."

(Ovid)

18th December

"Love nothing more but that which comes to you woven in the pattern of your destiny. For what could more aptly fit your needs?"

(Marcus Aurelius)

19th December

"Nurture your mind with great thoughts. To believe in the heroic makes heroes."

(Benjamin Disraeli)

20th December

"It is a mistake to look too far ahead. Only one link of the chain of destiny can be handled at a time."

(Winston Churchill)

21st December

"There is only one success – to be able to spend your life in your own way."

(Christopher Morley)

22nd December

"Adapt yourself to the life you have been given; and truly love the people with whom destiny has surrounded you."

(Marcus Aurelius)

23rd December

"Happy is the man who can do only one thing; in doing it, he fulfills his destiny."

(Joseph Joubert)

24th December

"If you don't know where you are going, you'll end up some place else."

(Confucius)

25th December

"The destiny of man is in his own soul."

(Herodotus)

26th December

"Our destiny can be examined, but it cannot be justified or totally explained. We are simply here."

(Iris Murdoch)

27th December

"The acts of this life are the destiny of the next. He hath no leisure who uses it not. He that will not reflect is a ruined man."

(Proverb)

28th December

"Every man has his own destiny; the only imperative is to follow it, to accept it, no matter where it leads him."

(Henry Miller)

29th December

"The tissue of life to be we weave with colors all our own; And in the field of destiny we reap as we have sown."

(John Greenleaf Whittier)

30th December

"Our destiny changes with our thoughts; we shall become what we wish to become, do what we wish to do, when our habitual thoughts correspond with our desires."

(Orison Swett Marden)

31st December

"Destiny is not a matter of chance; but a matter of choice. It is not a thing to be waited for, It is a thing to be achieved."

(William Jennings Bryan)

ABOUT THE AUTHOR

I am simply the collator of the quotes. The authors of the quotes are numerous and have all been listed in this book against their respective quotes.

21572093R00039

Printed in Great Britain
by Amazon